Classic Christmas

Stories, pictures and Christmas word puzzle games for the entire family

There is something storybook like about sparkles,
ribbons, baubles, tinsel and glitter ...
We all remember how we felt when we were small children
waiting on Santa ... and how the anticipation would grow
as Christmas day approached. That truly was such a
special feeling, which you now can recreate for the entire
family by reading classic Christmas stories and scrolling trough
authentic vintage Christmas images, while the younger
family members can partake in the joyful Christmas
games inside this book.

Classic Christmas Stories

LITTLE GIRL'S CHRISTMAS
WINNIFRED E. LINCOLN

It was Christmas Eve, and Little Girl had just hung up her stocking by the fireplace--right where it would be all ready for Santa when he slipped down the chimney. She knew he was coming, because--well, because it was Christmas Eve, and because he always had come to leave gifts for her on all the other Christmas Eves that she could remember, and because she had seen his pictures everywhere down town that afternoon when she was out with Mother.

STILL, she wasn't JUST satisfied. 'Way down in her heart she was a little uncertain--you see, when you have never really and truly seen a person with your very own eyes, it's hard to feel as if you exactly believed in him--even though that person always has left beautiful gifts for you every time he has come. "Oh, he'll come," said Little Girl; "I just know he will be here before morning, but somehow I wish--" "Well, what do you wish?" said a Tiny Voice close by her--so close that Little Girl fairly jumped when she heard it.

"Why, I wish I could SEE Santa myself. I'd just like to go and see his house and his workshop, and ride in his sleigh, and know Mrs. Santa—'it would be such fun, and then I'd KNOW for sure." "Why don't you go, then?" said Tiny Voice. "It's easy enough. Just try on these Shoes, and take this Light in your hand, and you'll find your way all right." So Little Girl looked down on the hearth, and there were two cunning little Shoes side by side, and a little Spark of a Light close to them--just as if they were all made out of one of the glowing coals of the wood-fire. Such cunning Shoes as they were--Little Girl could hardly wait to pull off her slippers and try them on.

They looked as if they were too small, but they weren't--they fitted exactly right, and just as Little Girl had put them both on and had taken the Light in her hand, along came a little Breath of Wind, and away she went up the chimney, along with ever so many other little Sparks, past the Soot Fairies, and out into the Open Air, where Jack Frost and the Star Beams were all busy at work making the world look pretty for Christmas.

Away went Little Girl--Two Shoes, Bright Light, and all--higher and higher, until she looked like a wee bit of a star up in the sky. It was the funniest thing, but she seemed to know the way perfectly, and didn't have to stop to make inquiries anywhere. You see it was a straight road all the way, and when one doesn't have to think about turning to the right or the left, it makes things very much easier. Pretty soon Little Girl noticed that there was a bright light all around her--oh, a very bright light--and right away something down in her heart began to make her feel very happy indeed. She didn't know that the Christmas spirits and little Christmas fairies were all around her and even right inside her, because she couldn't see a single one of them, even though her eyes were very bright and could usually see a great deal.

But that was just it, and Little Girl felt as if she wanted to laugh and sing and be glad. It made her remember the Sick Boy who lived next door, and she said to herself that she would carry him one of her prettiest picture-books in the morning, so that he could have something to make him happy all day. By and by, when the bright light all around her had grown very, very much brighter, Little Girl saw a path right in front of her, all straight and trim, leading up a hill to a big, big house with ever and ever so many windows in it.

When she had gone just a bit nearer, she saw candles in every window, red and green and yellow ones, and every one burning brightly, so Little Girl knew right away that these were Christmas candles to light her on her journey, and make the way dear for her, and something told her that this was Santa's house, and that pretty soon she would perhaps see Santa himself.

Just as she neared the steps and before she could possibly have had time to ring the bell, the door opened--opened of itself as wide as could be--and there stood--not Santa himself--don't think it--but a funny Little Man with slender little legs and a roly-poly stomach which shook every now and then when he laughed.

You would have known right away, just as Little Girl knew, that he was a very happy little man, and you would have guessed right away, too, that the reason he was so roly-poly was because he laughed and chuckled and smiled all the time--for it's only sour, cross folks who are thin and skimpy. Quick as a wink, he pulled off his little peaked red cap, smiled the broadest kind of a smile, and said, "Merry Christmas! Merry Christmas! Come in! Come in!"

So in went Little Girl, holding fast to Little Man's hand, and when she was really inside there was the jolliest, reddest fire all glowing and snapping, and there were Little Man and all his brothers and sisters, who said their names were "Merry Christmas," and "Good Cheer," and ever so many other jolly-sounding things, and there were such a lot of them that Little Girl just knew she never could count them, no matter how long she tried.

All around her were bundles and boxes and piles of toys and games, and Little Girl knew that these were all ready and waiting to be loaded into Santa's big sleigh for his reindeer to whirl them away over cloud tops and snowdrifts to the little people down below who had left their stockings all ready for him. Pretty soon all the little Good Cheer Brothers began to hurry and bustle and carry out the bundles as fast as they could to the steps where Little Girl could hear the jingling bells and the stamping of hoofs.

So Little Girl picked up some bundles and skipped along too, for she wanted to help a bit herself--it's no fun whatever at Christmas unless you can help, you know--and there in the yard stood the BIGGEST sleigh that Little Girl had ever seen, and the reindeer were all stamping and prancing and jingling the bells on their harnesses, because they were so eager to be on their way to the Earth once more.

She could hardly wait for Santa to come, and just as she had begun to wonder where he was, the door opened again and out came a whole forest of Christmas trees, at least it looked just as if a whole forest had started out for a walk somewhere, but a second glance

showed Little Girl that there were thousands of Christmas sprites, and that each one carried a tree or a big Christmas wreath on his back. Behind them all, she could hear some one laughing loudly, and talking in a big, jovial voice that sounded as if he were good friends with the whole world.

AND STRAIGHTWAY she knew that Santa himself was coming. Little Girl's heart went pit-a-pat for a minute while she wondered if Santa would notice her, but she didn't have to wonder long, for he spied her at once and said: "Bless my soul! who's this? and where did you come from?"

LITTLE GIRL THOUGHT PERHAPS she might be afraid to answer him, but she wasn't one bit afraid. You see he had such a kind little twinkle in his eyes that she felt happy right away as she replied, "Oh, I'm Little Girl, and I wanted so much to see Santa that I just came, and here I am!"

"HO, HO, HO, HO, HO!" laughed Santa, "and here you are! Wanted to see Santa, did you, and so you came! Now that's very nice, and it's too bad I'm in such a hurry, for we should like nothing better than to show you about and give you a real good time. But you see it is quarter of twelve now, and I must be on my way at once, else I'll never reach that first chimney-top by midnight. I'd call Mrs. Santa and ask her to get you some supper, but she is busy finishing dolls' clothes which must be done before morning, and I guess we'd better not bother her.

Is THERE anything that you would like, Little Girl?" and good old Santa put his big warm hand on Little Girl's curls and she felt its warmth and kindness clear down to her very heart. You see, my dears, that even though Santa was in such a great hurry, he wasn't too busy to stop and make some one happy for a minute, even if it was some one no bigger than Little Girl.

So she smiled back into Santa's face and said: "Oh, Santa, if I could ONLY ride down to Earth with you behind those splendid reindeer! I'd love to go; won't you PLEASE take me? I'm so small that I won't take up much room on the seat, and I'll keep very still and not bother one bit!"

Then Santa laughed, SUCH a laugh, big and loud and rollicking, and he said, "Wants a ride, does she? Well, well, shall we take her, Little Elves? Shall we take her, Little Fairies? Shall we take her, Good Reindeer?"

And all the Little Elves hopped and skipped and brought Little Girl a sprig of holly; and all the Little Fairies bowed and smiled and brought her a bit of mistletoe; and all the Good Reindeer jingled their bells loudly, which meant, "Oh, yes! let's take her! She's a good Little Girl! Let her ride!" And before Little Girl could even think, she found herself all tucked up in the big fur robes beside Santa, and away they went, right out into the air, over the clouds, through the Milky Way, and right under the very handle of the Big Dipper, on, on, toward the Earth land, whose lights Little Girl began to see twinkling away down below her. Presently she felt the runners scrape upon something, and she knew they must be on some one's roof, and that Santa would slip down some one's chimney in a minute.

. . .

How she wanted to go, too! You see if you had never been down a chimney and seen Santa fill up the stockings, you would want to go quite as much as Little Girl did, now, wouldn't you? So, just as Little Girl was wishing as hard as ever she could wish, she heard a Tiny Voice say, "Hold tight to his arm! Hold tight to his arm!" So she held Santa's arm tight and close, and he shouldered his pack, never thinking that it was heavier than usual, and with a bound and a slide, there they were, Santa, Little Girl, pack and all, right in the middle of a room where there was a fireplace and stockings all hung up for Santa to fill.

Just then Santa noticed Little Girl. He had forgotten all about her for a minute, and he was very much surprised to find that she had come, too. "Bless my soul!" he said, "where did you come from, Little Girl? and how in the world can we both get back up that chimney again? It's easy enough to slide down, but it's quite another matter to climb up again!" and Santa looked real worried.

But Little Girl was beginning to feel very tired by this time, for she had had a very exciting evening, so she said, "Oh, never mind me, Santa. I've had such a good time, and I'd just as soon stay here a while as not. I believe I'll curl up on his hearth-rug a few minutes and have a little nap, for it looks as warm and cozy as our own hearth-rug at home, and--why, it is our own hearth and it's my own nursery, for there is Teddy Bear in his chair where I leave him every night, and there's Bunny Cat curled up on his cushion in the corner.

And Little Girl turned to thank Santa and say goodbye to him, but either he had gone very quickly, or else she had fallen asleep very quickly--she never could tell which--for the next thing she knew, Daddy was holding her in his arms and was saying, "What is my

Little Girl doing here? She must go to bed, for it's Christmas Eve, and old Santa won't come if he thinks there are any little folks about."

But Little Girl knew better than that, and when she began to tell him all about it, and how the Christmas fairies had welcomed her, and how Santa had given her such a fine ride, Daddy laughed and laughed, and said, "You've been dreaming, Little Girl, you've been dreaming." But Little Girl knew better than that, too, for there on the hearth was the little Black Coal, which had given her Two Shoes and Bright Light, and tight in her hand she held a holly berry which one of the Christmas Sprites had placed there.

More than all that, there she was on the hearth-rug herself, just as Santa had left her, and that was the best proof of all. The trouble was, Daddy himself had never been a Little Girl, so he couldn't tell anything about it, but we know she hadn't been dreaming, now, don't we, my dears?

Toinette and the Elves

Susan Coolidge

The winter's sun was nearing the horizon's edge. Each moment the tree shadows grew longer in the forest; each moment the crimson light on the upper boughs became more red and bright. It was Christmas Eve, or would be in half an hour, when the sun should be fairly set; but it did not feel like Christmas, for the afternoon was mild and sweet, and the wind in the leafless boughs sang, as it moved about, as though to imitate the vanished birds. Soft trills and whistles, odd little shakes and twitters--it was astonishing what pretty noises the wind made, for it was in good humour, as winds should be on the Blessed Night; all its storm-tones and bass-notes were for the moment laid aside, and gently as though hushing a baby to sleep, it cooed and rustled and brushed to and fro in the leafless woods.

Toinette stood, pitcher in hand, beside the well. "Wishing Well," the people called it, for they believed that if any one standing there bowed to the East, repeated a certain rhyme and wished a wish, the wish would certainly come true.

Unluckily, nobody knew exactly what the rhyme should be. Toinette did not; she was wishing that she did, as she stood with her eyes fixed on the bubbling water. How nice it would be! she thought. What beautiful things should be hers, if it were only to wish and to have. She would be beautiful, rich, good--oh, so good. The children should love her dearly, and never be disagreeable. Mother should not work so hard--they should all go back to France--which mother said was si belle. Oh, dear, how nice it would be. Meantime, the sun sank lower, and mother at home was waiting for the water, but Toinette forgot that.

Suddenly she started. A low sound of crying met her ear, and something like a tiny moan. It seemed close by but she saw nothing Hastily she filled her pitcher and turned to go. But again the sound came, an unmistakable sob, right under her feet. Toinette stopped short. "What is the matter?" she called out bravely. "Is anybody there? and if there is, why don't I see you?"

A third sob--and all at once, down on the ground beside her, a tiny figure became visible, so small that Toinette had to kneel and stoop her head to see it plainly. The figure was that of an odd little man. He wore a garb of green bright and glancing as the scales of a beetle. In his mite of a hand was a cap, out of which stuck a long pointed feather. Two specks of tears stood on his cheeks and he fixed on Toinette a glance so sharp and so sad that it made her feel sorry and frightened and confused all at once. "Why how funny this is!" she said, speaking to herself out loud. "Not at all," replied the little man, in a voice as dry and crisp as the chirr of a grasshopper. "Anything but funny. I wish you wouldn't use such words. It hurts my feelings, Toinette."

"Do you know my name, then?" cried Toinette, astonished. "That's strange. But what is the matter? Why are you crying so, little man?" "I'm not a little man. I'm an elf," responded the dry voice; "and I think you'd cry if you had an engagement out to tea, and found yourself spiked on a great bayonet, so that you couldn't move an inch. Look!" He turned a little as he spoke and Toinette saw a long rose-thorn sticking through the back of the green robe. The little man could by no means reach the thorn, and it held him fast prisoner to the place.

"Is that all? I'll take it out for you," she said. "Be careful--oh, be careful," entreated the little man. "This is my new dress, you know--my Christmas suit, and it's got to last a year. If there is a hole in it, Peascod will tickle me and Bean Blossom tease, till I shall wish myself dead." He stamped with vexation at the thought. "Now, you mustn't do that," said Toinette, in a motherly tone, "else you'll tear it yourself, you know." She broke off the thorn as she spoke, and gently drew it out. The elf anxiously examined the stuff. A tiny puncture only was visible and his face brightened. "You're a good child," he said. "I'll do as much for you some day, perhaps." "I would have come before if I had seen you," remarked Toinette, timidly. "But I didn't see you a bit."

"No, because I had my cap on," cried the elf. He placed it on his head as he spoke, and hey, presto! nobody was there, only a voice which laughed and said: "Well--don't stare so. Lay your finger on me now."
"Oh," said Toinette, with a gasp. "How wonderful. What fun it must be to do that. The children wouldn't see me. I should steal in and surprise them; they would go on talking, and never guess that I was there. I should so like it.

Do elves ever lend their caps to anybody? I wish you'd lend me yours. It must be so nice to be invisible." "Ho," cried the elf, appearing suddenly again. "Lend my cap, indeed! Why it wouldn't stay on the very tip of your ear, it's so small. As for nice, that depends. Sometimes it is, and sometimes it isn't. No, the only way for mortal people to be invisible is to gather the fern-seed and put it in their shoes." "Gather it? Where? I never saw any seed to the ferns," said Toinette, staring about her.

"Of course not--we elves take care of that," replied the little man. "Nobody finds the fern-seed but ourselves. I'll tell you what, though. You were such a nice child to take out the thorn so cleverly, that I'll give you a little of the seed. Then you can try the fun of being invisible, to your heart's content.""Will you really? How delightful. May I have it now?"

"Bless me. Do you think I carry my pockets stuffed with it?" said the elf. "Not at all. Go home, say not a word to any one, but leave your bedroom window open to night, and you'll see what you'll see."He laid his finger on his nose as he spoke, gave a jump like a grasshopper, clapping on his cap as he went, and vanished. Toinette lingered a moment, in hopes that he might come back, then took her pitcher and hurried home. The woods were very dusky by this time; but full of her strange adventures, she did not remember to feel afraid.

"How long you have been," said her mother. "It's late for a little maid like you to be up. You must make better speed another time, my child."

Toinette pouted as she was apt to do when reproved. The children clamoured to know what had kept her, and she spoke pettishly and crossly; so that they too became cross, and presently went away into the outer kitchen to play by themselves. The children were apt to creep away when Toinette came. It made her angry and unhappy at times that they should do so, but she did not realize that it was in great part her own fault, and so did not set herself to mend it.

"Tell me a 'tory," said baby Jeanneton, creeping to her knee a little later. But Toinette's head was full of the elf; she had no time to spare for Jeanneton. "Oh, not to-night," she replied. "Ask mother to tell you one.""Mother's busy," said Jeanneton wistfully.Toinette took no notice and the little one crept away disconsolately. Bedtime at last. Toinette set the casement open, and lay a long time waiting and watching; then she fell asleep. She waked with a sneeze and jump and sat up in bed. Behold, on the coverlet stood her elfin friend, with a long train of other elves beside him, all clad in the beetle-wing green, and wearing little pointed caps. More were coming in at the window; outside a few were drifting about in the moon rays, which lit their sparkling robes till they glittered like so many fireflies. The odd thing was, that though the caps were on, Toinette could see the elves distinctly and this surprised her so much, that again she thought out loud and said, "How funny."

"You mean about the caps," replied her special elf, who seemed to have the power of reading thought. "Yes, you can see us to-night, caps and all. Spells lose their value on Christmas Eve, always. Peas-cod, where is the box? Do you still wish to try the experiment of being invisible, Toinette?" "Oh, yes--indeed I do." "Very well; so let it be." As he spoke he beckoned, and two elves puffing and panting like little men with a heavy load, dragged forward a droll little box about the size of a pumpkin-seed.

One of them lifted the cover.

"Pay the porter, please, ma'am," he said giving Toinette's ear a mischievous tweak with his sharp fingers. "Hands off, you bad Peascod!" cried Toinette's elf. "This is my girl. She shan't be pinched!" He dealt Peascod a blow with his tiny hand as he spoke and looked so brave and warlike that he seemed at least an inch taller than he had before. Toinette admired him very much; and Peascod slunk away with an abashed giggle muttering that Thistle needn't be so ready with his fist.

Thistle--for thus, it seemed, Toinette's friend was named--dipped his fingers in the box, which was full of fine brown seeds, and shook a handful into each of Toinette's shoes, as they stood, toes together by the bedside. "Now you have your wish," he said, and can go about and do what you like, no one seeing. The charm will end at sunset. Make the most of it while you can; but if you want to end it sooner, shake the seeds from the shoes and then you are just as usual." "Oh, I shan't want to," protested Toinette; "I'm sure I shan't."

"Good-bye," said Thistle, with a mocking little laugh. "Good-bye, and thank you ever so much," replied Toinette. "Good-bye, good-bye," replied the other elves, in shrill chorus. They clustered together, as if in consultation; then straight out of the window they flew like a swarm of gauzy-winged bees, and melted into the moonlight. Toinette jumped up and ran to watch them but the little men were gone--not a trace of them was to be seen; so she shut the window, went back to bed and presently in the midst of her amazed and excited thoughts fell asleep.

She waked in the morning, with a queer, doubtful feeling. Had she dreamed, or had it really happened? She put on her best petticoat and laced her blue bodice; for she thought the mother would perhaps take them across the wood to the little chapel for the Christmas service. Her long hair smoothed and tied, her shoes trimly fastened, downstairs she ran. The mother was stirring porridge over the fire. Toinette went close to her, but she did not move or turn her head.

"How late the children are," she said at last, lifting the boiling pot on the hob. Then she went to the stair-foot and called, "Marc, Jeanneton, Pierre, Marie. Breakfast is ready, my children. Toinette--but where, then, is Toinette? She is used to be down long before this.""Toinette isn't upstairs," said Marie from above."Her door is wide open, and she isn't there.""That is strange," said the mother. "I have been here an hour, and she has not passed this way since." She went to the outer door and called, "Toinette! Toinette!" passing close to Toinette as she did so. And looking straight at her with unseeing eyes. Toinette, half frightened, half pleased, giggled low to herself. She really was invisible, then. How strange it seemed and what fun it was going to be.

The children sat down to breakfast, little Jeanneton, as the youngest, saying grace. The mother distributed the porridge and gave each a spoon but she looked anxious. "Where can Toinette have gone?" she said to herself. Toinette was conscious-pricked. She was half inclined to dispel the charm on the spot. But just then she caught a whisper from Pierre to Marc which so surprised her as to put the idea out of her head. "Perhaps a wolf has eaten her up--a great big wolf like the 'Capuchon Rouge,' you know." This was what Pierre said; and Marc answered unfeelingly:

"If he has, I shall ask mother to let me have her room for my own." Poor Toinette, her cheeks burned and her eyes filled with tears at this. Didn't the boys love her a bit then? Next she grew angry, and longed to box Marc's ears, only she recollected in time that she was invisible. What a bad boy he was, she thought.

The smoking porridge reminded her that she was hungry; so brushing away the tears she slipped a spoon off the table and whenever she found the chance, dipped it into the bowl for a mouthful. The porridge disappeared rapidly. "I want some more," said Jeanneton. "Bless me, how fast you have eaten," said the mother, turning to the bowl. This made Toinette laugh, which shook her spoon, and a drop of the hot mixture fell right on the tip of Marie's nose as she sat with upturned face waiting her turn for a second helping. Marie gave a little scream. "What is it?" said the mother. "Hot water! Right in my face!" sputtered Marie. "Water!" cried Marc. "It's porridge."

"You spattered with your spoon. Eat more carefully, my child," said the mother, and Toinette laughed again as she heard her. After all, there was some fun in being invisible. The morning went by. Constantly the mother went to the door, and, shading her eyes with her hand, looked out, in hopes of seeing a little figure come down the wood-path, for she thought perhaps the child went to the spring after water, and fell asleep there.

The children played happily, meanwhile. They were used to doing without Toinette and did not seem to miss her, except that now and then baby Jeanneton said: "Poor Toinette gone--not here--all gone."

"Well, what if she has?" said Marc at last looking up from the wooden cup he was carving for Marie's doll. "We can play all the better." Marc was a bold, outspoken boy, who always told his whole mind about things

"If she were here," he went on," she'd only scold and interfere. Toinette almost always scolds. I like to have her go away. It makes it pleasanter." "It is rather pleasanter," admitted Marie, "only I'd like her to be having a nice time somewhere else." "Bother about Toinette," cried Pierre. "Let's play 'My godmother has cabbage to sell.'" I don't think Toinette had ever felt so unhappy in her life, as when she stood by unseen, and heard the children say these words. She had never meant to be unkind to them, but she was quick tempered, dreamy, wrapped up in herself.

She did not like being interrupted by them, it put her out, and she spoke sharply and was cross. She had taken it for granted that the others must love her, by a sort of right, and the knowledge that they did not grieved over very much. Creeping away, she hid herself in the woods. It was a sparkling day, but the sun did not look so bright as usual. Cuddled down under a rosebush, Toinette sat sobbing as if her heart would break at the recollection of the speeches she had overheard.

By and by a little voice within her woke up and began to make itself audible. All of us know this little voice. We call it conscience. "Jeanneton missed me," she thought. "And, oh, dear! I pushed her away only last night and wouldn't tell her a story. And Marie hoped I was having a pleasant time somewhere. I wish I hadn't slapped Marie last Friday. And I wish I hadn't thrown Marc's ball into the fire that day I was angry with him. How unkind he was to say that--but I

wasn't always kind to him. And once I said that I wished a bear would eat Pierre up. That was because he broke my cup. Oh, dear, oh, dear. What a bad girl I've been to them all."

"But you could be better and kinder if you tried, couldn't you?" said the inward voice. "I think you could." And Toinette clasped her hands tight and said out loud: "I could. Yes--and I will."

The first thing to be done was to get rid of the fern-seed which she now regarded as a hateful thing. She untied her shoes and shook it out in the grass. It dropped and seemed to melt into the air, for it instantly vanished. A mischievous laugh sounded close behind, and a beetle-green coat-tail was visible whisking under a tuft of rushes. But Toinette had had enough of the elves, and, tying her shoes, took the road toward home, running with all her might."Where have you been all day, Toinette?" cried the children, as, breathless and panting, she flew in at the gate. But Toinette could not speak. She made slowly for her mother, who stood in the doorway, flung herself into her arms and burst into a passion of tears.

"Ma cherie, what is it, whence hast thou come?" asked the good mother alarmed. She lifted Toinette into her arms as she spoke, and hastened indoors. The other children followed, whispering and peeping, but the mother sent them away, and sitting down by the fire with Toinette in her lap, she rocked and hushed and comforted, as though Toinette had been again a little baby. Gradually the sobs ceased. For a while Toinette lay quiet, with her head on her mother's breast. Then she wiped her wet eyes, put her arms around her mother's neck, and told her all from the very beginning, keeping not a single thing back. The dame listened with alarm.

"Saints protect us," she muttered. Then feeling Toinette's hands and head, "Thou hast a fever," she said. "I will make thee a tisane, my darling, and thou must at once go to bed." Toinette vainly protested;to bed she went and perhaps it was the wisest thing, for the warm drink threw her into a long sound sleep and when she woke she was herself again, bright and well, hungry for dinner, and ready to do her usual tasks.

Herself--but not quite the same Toinette that she had been before. Nobody changes from bad to better in a minute. It takes time for that, time and effort, and a long struggle with evil habits and tempers. But there is sometimes a certain minute or day in which people begin to change, and thus it was with Toinette. The fairy lesson was not lost upon her. She began to fight with herself, to watch her faults and try to conquer them. It was hard work; often she felt discouraged, but she kept on. Week after week and month after month she grew less selfish, kinder, more obliging than she used to be. When she failed and her old fractious temper got the better of her, she was sorry and begged every one's pardon so humbly that they could not but forgive. The mother began to think that the elves really had bewitched her child.

As for the children they learned to love Toinette as never before, and came to her with all their pains and pleasures, as children should to a kind older sister. Each fresh proof of this, every kiss from Jeanneton, every confidence from Marc, was a comfort to Toinette, for she never forgot Christmas Day, and felt that no trouble was too much to wipe out that unhappy recollection. "I think they like me better than they did then," she would say; but then the thought came, "Perhaps if I were invisible again, if they did not know I was there, I might hear something to make me feel as badly as I did that morning." These sad thoughts were part of the bitter fruit of the fairy fern-seed.

So with doubts and fears the year went by, and again it was Christmas Eve. Toinette had been asleep some hours when she was roused by a sharp tapping at the window pane. Startled, and only half awake, she sat up in bed and saw by the moonlight a tiny figure outside which she recognized. It was Thistle drumming with his knuckles on the glass.

"Let me in," cried the dry little voice. So Toinette opened the casement, and Thistle flew in and perched as before on the coverlet. "Merry Christmas, my girl." he said, "and a Happy New Year when it comes. I've brought you a present;" and, dipping into a pouch tied round his waist, he pulled out a handful of something brown. Toinette knew what it was in a moment. "Oh, no," she cried shrinking back. "Don't give me any fern-seeds. They frighten me. I don't like them."

"Don't be silly," said Thistle, his voice sounding kind this time, and earnest. "It wasn't pleasant being invisible last year, but perhaps this year it will be. Take my advice, and try it. You'll not be sorry." "Sha'n't I?" said Toinette, brightening. "Very well, then, I will." She leaned out of bed, and watched Thistle strew the fine dustlike grains in each shoe. "I'll drop in to-morrow night, and just see how you like it," he said. Then, with a nod, he was gone. The old fear came back when she woke in the morning, and she tied on her shoes with a tremble at her heart. Downstairs she stole. The first thing she saw was a wooden ship standing on her plate. Marc had made the ship, but Toinette had no idea it was for her.

. . .

THE LITTLE ONES sat round the table with their eyes on the door, watching till Toinette should come in and be surprised. "I wish she'd hurry," said Pierre, drumming on his bowl with a spoon. "We all want Toinette, don't we?" said the mother, smiling as she poured the hot porridge. "It will be fun to see her stare," declared Marc. "Toinette is jolly when she stares. Her eyes look big and her cheeks grow pink. Andre Brugen thinks his sister Aline is prettiest, but I don't. Our Toinette is ever so pretty."

"SHE IS EVER SO NICE, TOO," said Pierre. "She's as good to play with as--as--a boy," finished triumphantly. "Oh, I wish my Toinette would come," said Jeanneton. Toinette waited no longer, but sped upstairs with glad tears in her eyes. Two minutes, and down she came again visible this time. Her heart was light as a feather. "Merry Christmas!" clamoured the children. The ship was presented, Toinette was duly surprised, and so the happy day began. That night Toinette left the window open, and lay down in her clothes; for she felt, as Thistle had been so kind, she ought to receive him politely. He came at midnight, and with him all the other little men in green.

"WELL, HOW WAS IT?" asked Thistle. "Oh, I liked it this time," declared Toinette, with shining eyes, "and I thank you so much." "I'm glad you did," said the elf. "And I'm glad you are thankful, for we want you to do something for us." "What can it be?" inquired Toinette, wondering. "You must know," went on Thistle, "that there is no dainty in the world which we elves enjoy like a bowl of fern-seed broth. But it has to be cooked over a real fire, and we dare not go near fire, you know, lest our wings scorch. So we seldom get any fern-seed broth.

Now, Toinette, will you make us some?" "Indeed, I will!" cried Toinette, "only you must tell me how." "It is very simple," said Peascod; "only seed and honey dew, stirred from left to right with a sprig of fennel. Here's the seed and the fennel, and here's the dew. Be sure and stir from the left; if you don't, it curdles, and the flavour will be spoiled."

Down into the kitchen they went, and Toinette, moving very softly quickened the fire, set on the smallest bowl she could find, and spread the doll's table with the wooden saucers which Marc had made for Jeanneton to play with. Then she mixed and stirred as the elves bade, and when the soup was done, served it to them smoking hot. How they feasted! No bumblebee, dipping into a flower-cup, ever sipped and twinkled more rapturously than they.

When the last drop was eaten, they made ready to go. Each in turn kissed Toinette's hand, and said a word of farewell. Thistle brushed his feathered cap over the doorpost as he passed."Be lucky, house," he said, "for you have received and entertained the luck-bringers. And be lucky, Toinette. Good temper is good luck, and

sweet words and kind looks and peace in the heart are the fairest of fortunes. See that you never lose them again, my girl." With this, he, too, kissed Toinette's hand, waved his feathered cap, and--whir! they all were gone, while Toinette, covering the fire with ashes and putting aside the little cups, stole up to her bed a happy child.

A CHRISTMAS FAIRY

JOHN STRANGE WINTER

It was getting very near to Christmas time, and all the boys at Miss Ware's school were talking about going home for the holidays.

"I shall go to the Christmas festival," said Bertie Fellows," and my mother will have a party, and my Aunt will give another. Oh! I shall have a splendid time at home." "My Uncle Bob is going to give me a pair of skates," remarked Harry Wadham. "My father is going to give me a bicycle," put in George Alderson.

"Will you bring it back to school with you?" asked Harry. "Oh! yes, if Miss Ware doesn't say no." "Well, Tom," cried Bertie, "where are you going to spend your holidays?" "I am going to stay here," answered Tom in a very forlorn voice. "Here--at school--oh, dear! Why can't you go home?"

"I can't go home to India," answered Tom. "Nobody said you could. But haven't you any relatives anywhere?" Tom shook his head. "Only in India," he said sadly. "Poor fellow! That's hard luck for you. I'll tell you what it is, boys, if I couldn't go home for the holidays, especially at Christmas--I think I would just sit down and die."

"Oh, no, you wouldn't," said Tom. "You would get ever so homesick, but you wouldn't die. You would just get through somehow, and hope something would happen before next year, or that some kind fairy would--" "There are no fairies nowadays," said Bertie. "See here, Tom, I'll write and ask my mother to invite you to go home with me for the holidays." "Will you really?"

"Yes, I will. And if she says yes, we shall have such a splendid time. We live in London, you know, and have lots of parties and fun." "Perhaps she will say no?" suggested poor little Tom. "My mother isn't the kind that says no," Bertie declared loudly.

In a few days' time a letter arrived from Bertie's mother. The boy opened it eagerly. It said: My own dear Bertie: I am very sorry to tell you that little Alice is ill with scarlet fever. And so you cannot come for your holidays. I would have been glad to have you bring your little friend with you if all had been well here.

Your father and I have decided that the best thing that you can do is to stay at Miss Ware's. We shall send your Christmas present to you as well as we can.

It will not be like coming home, but I am sure you will try to be happy, and make me feel that you are helping me in this sad time. Dear little Alice is very ill, very ill indeed. Tell Tom that I am sending you a box for both of you, with two of everything. And tell him that it makes me so much happier to know that you will not be alone.

When Bertie Fellows received this letter, which ended all his Christmas hopes and joys, he hid his face upon his desk and sobbed aloud. The lonely boy from India, who sat next to him, tried to comfort his friend in every way he could think of. He patted his shoulder and whispered many kind words to him. At last Bertie put the letter into Tom's hands. "Read it," he sobbed.

So then Tom understood the cause of Bertie's grief. "Don't fret over it," he said at last. "It might be worse. Why, your father and mother might be thousands of miles away, like mine are. When Alice is better, you will be able to go home. And it will help your mother if she thinks you are almost as happy as if you could go now." Soon Miss Ware came to tell Bertie how sorry she was for him.

"After all," said she, smiling down on the two boys, "it is an ill wind that blows nobody good. Poor Tom has been expecting to spend his holidays alone, and now he will have a friend with him--Try to look on the bright side, Bertie, and to remember how much worse it would have been if there had been no boy to stay with you."

"I can't help being disappointed, Miss Ware," said Bertie, his eyes filling with tears. "No; you would be a strange boy if you were not. But I want you to try to think of your poor mother, and write her as cheerfully as you can."

"Yes," answered Bertie; but his heart was too full to say more. The last day of the term came, and one by one, or two by two, the boys went away, until only Bertie and Tom were left in the great house. It had never seemed so large to either of them before.

"It's miserable," groaned poor Bertie, as they strolled into the schoolroom. "Just think if we were on our way home now--how different." "Just think if I had been left here by myself," said Tom. "Yes," said Bertie, "but you know when one wants to go home he never thinks of the boys that have no home to go to."

The evening passed, and the two boys went to bed. They told stories to each other for a long time before they could go to sleep. That night they dreamed of their homes, and felt very lonely. Yet each tried to be brave, and so another day began.

This was the day before Christmas. Quite early in the morning came the great box of which Bertie's mother had spoken in her letter. Then, just as dinner had come to an end, there was a peal of the bell, and a voice was heard asking for Tom Egerton. Tom sprang to his feet, and flew to greet a tall, handsome lady, crying, "Aunt Laura! Aunt Laura!"

And Laura explained that she and her husband had arrived in London only the day before. "I was so afraid, Tom," she said, "that we should not get here until Christmas Day was over and that you would be disappointed. So I would not let your mother write you that we were on our way home.

You must get your things packed up at once, and go back with me to London. Then uncle and I will give you a splendid time." For a minute or two Tom's face shone with delight. Then he caught sight of Bertie and turned to his aunt. "Dear Aunt Laura," he said, "I am very sorry, but I can't go." "Can't go? and why not?"

"Because I can't go and leave Bertie here all alone," he said stoutly. "When I was going to be alone he wrote and asked his mother to let me go home with him. She could not have either of us because Bertie's sister has scarlet fever. He has to stay here, and he has never been away from home at Christmas time before, and I can't go away and leave him by himself, Aunt Laura." For a minute Aunt Laura looked at the boy as if she could not believe him. Then she caught him in her arms and kissed him.

"You dear little boy, you shall not leave him. You shall bring him along, and we shall all enjoy ourselves together. Bertie, my boy, you are not very old yet, but I am going to teach you a lesson as well as I can. It is that kindness is never wasted in this world." And so Bertie and Tom found that there was such a thing as a fair after all.

Christmas Puzzles, Games & Authentic Pictures

CHRISTMAS
— crossword puzzle —

ANSWER: 1.Snowglobe 2.Deer 3.Present 4.Snowman 5.Stocking 6.Santa

WINTER
wordsearch puzzle

```
P E N G U I N B S B
F M P O B S R E C U
R A C N E M F A H L
O F C S U O A R O L
L H O O N N L U Q F
L C R S C K E Y A I
A M A U L N F I U N
S Q U I R R E L Q C
O R C O U I H F M H
U D E E R L A R E U
```

Find animals in the picture and in the puzzle

LLAMA   HARE
DEER   RACCOON
BEAR   MONKEY
PENGUIN SQUIRREL
BULLFINCH

ANSWER

CHRISTMAS Crossword

1 - santa; 2 - bear; 3 - tree; 4 - angel; 5 - elf; 6 - candycane

Word Puzzle Game

E	I	S	N	O	W	F	S	O	C	N
K	O	S	E	K	A	L	P	O	P	O
S	L	I	G	W	F	S	O	B	A	G
A	E	L	F	E	L	K	C	S	N	O
N	G	H	T	T	G	I	N	G	E	S
T	A	D	E	D	A	E	R	B	R	O
C	M	R	E	L	S	T	O	C	A	T
A	I	K	I	O	L	L	I	P	O	H
P	R	E	S	S	P	R	O	M	P	G
B	R	D	E	N	T	U	C	E	W	I
S	A	H	T	A	H	O	U	S	E	S

1. Santa 2. Spruce 3. Present 4. Elf 5. Sock 6. Snowflakes
7. Houses 8. Deer 9. Gingerbread 10. Bag 11. Lollipop

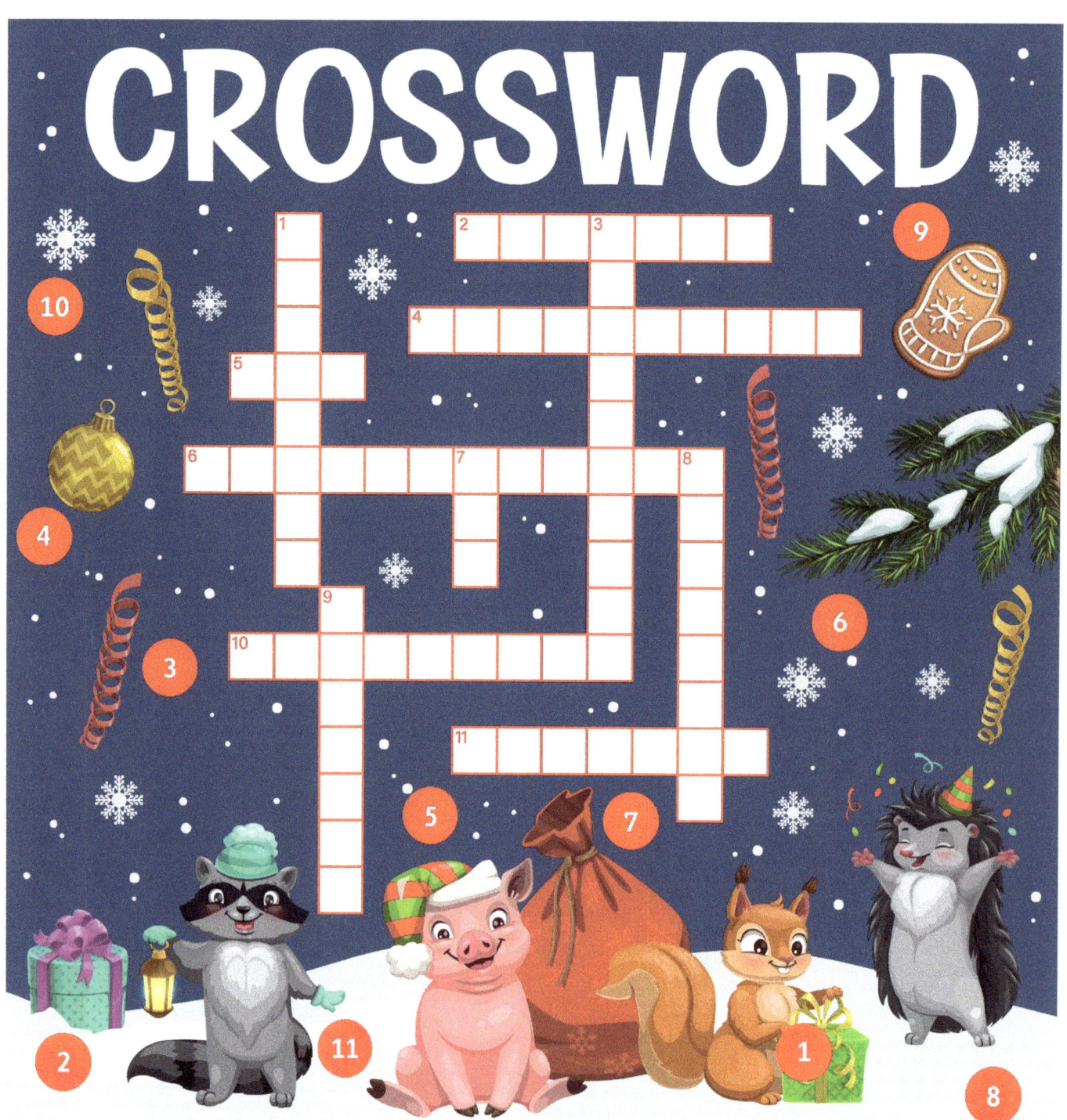

CHRISTMAS Crossword

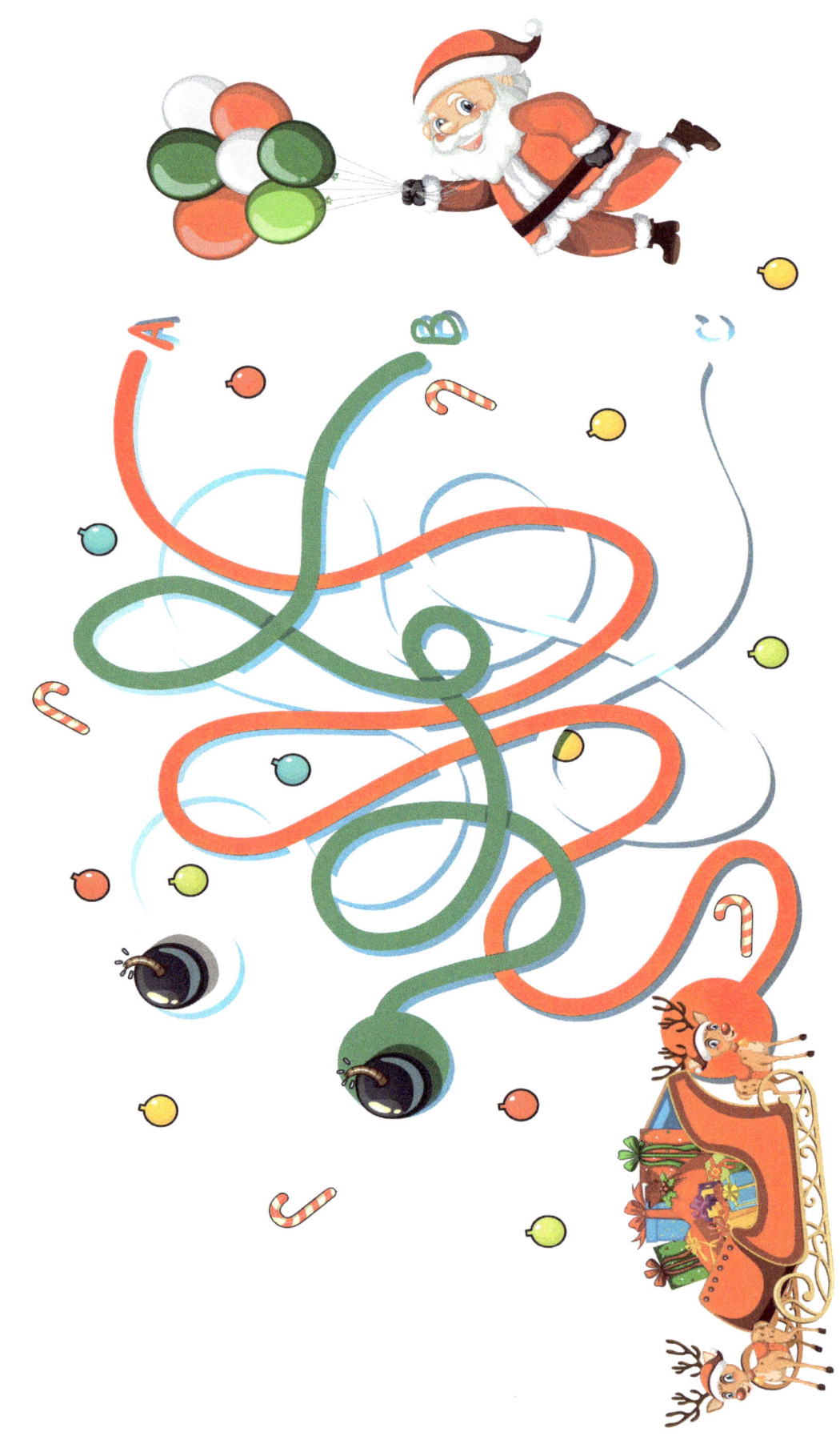

Find 10 Differences

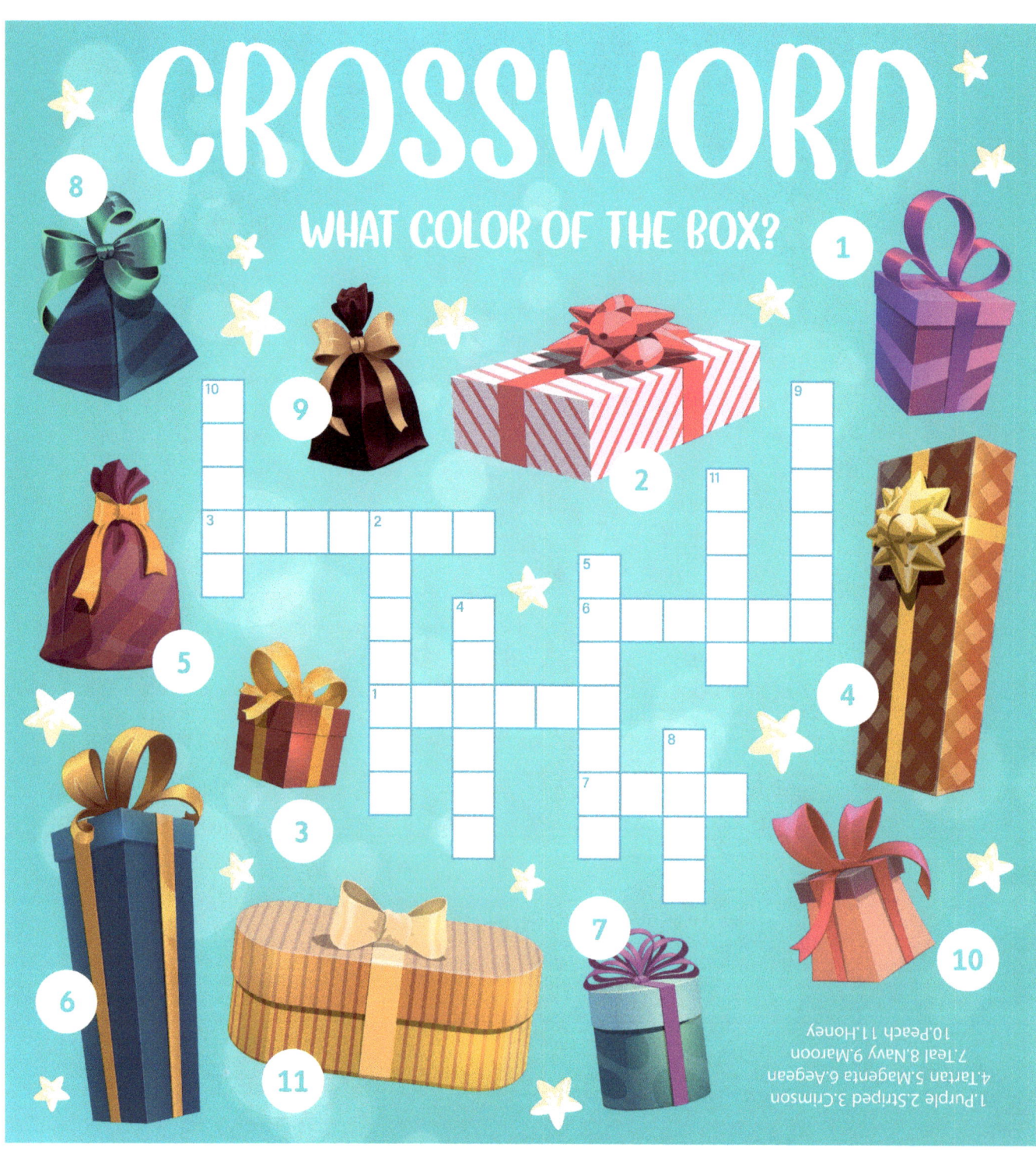

It's a Joy to Greet You on Christmas

WINTER THINGS
crossword puzzle

ANSWER: 1.Snowflake 1.↑Snowman 2.Hat 3.Boot 4.Scarf 5.Tea 6.Cacao 7.Earmuffs 8.Mitten 9.Sweater

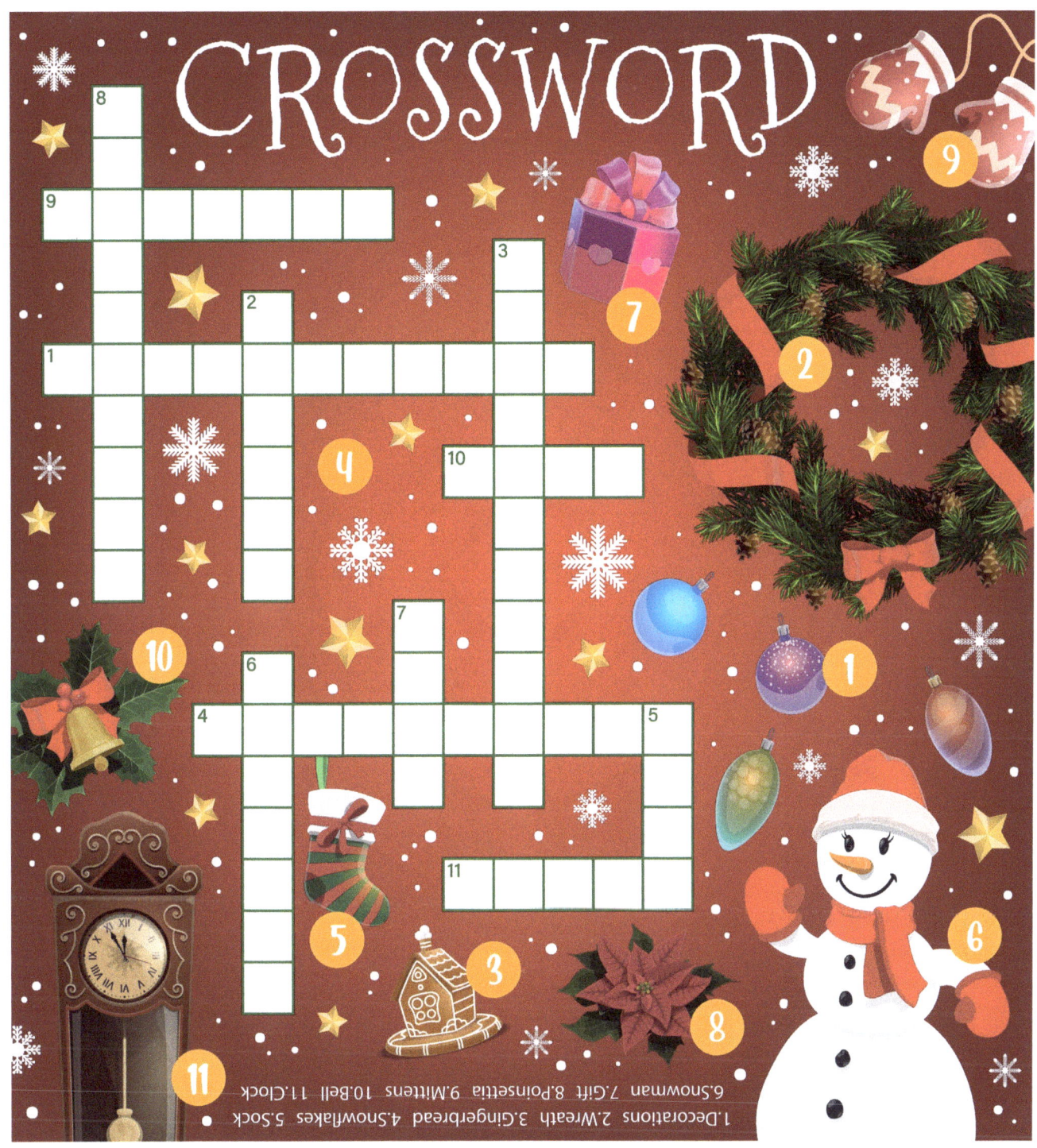

1.Decorations 2.Wreath 3.Gingerbread 4.Snowflakes 5.Sock 6.Snowman 7.Gift 8.Poinsettia 9.Mittens 10.Bell 11.Clock

Find 10 Differences

More Christmas themes books by Julia Brook

www.ingramcontent.com/pod-product-compliance
Lightning Source LLC
LaVergne TN
LVHW070532070526
838199LV00075B/6768

9799466124153